James Duff Brown

A Handbook of Library Appliances

The Technical Equipment of Libraries

James Duff Brown

A Handbook of Library Appliances
The Technical Equipment of Libraries

ISBN/EAN: 9783744644822

Printed in Europe, USA, Canada, Australia, Japan

Cover: Foto ©Andreas Hilbeck / pixelio.de

More available books at **www.hansebooks.com**

The Library Association Series

EDITED BY J. Y. W. MacALISTER AND THOMAS MASON
HON. SECRETARIES OF THE ASSOCIATION

No. 1.

A HANDBOOK OF
LIBRARY APPLIANCES:

THE

TECHNICAL EQUIPMENT OF LIBRARIES:

FITTINGS, FURNITURE, CHARGING SYSTEMS, FORMS, RECIPES
&c.

BY

JAMES D. BROWN
CLERKENWELL PUBLIC LIBRARY, LONDON

PUBLISHED FOR THE ASSOCIATION BY DAVID STOTT
370 OXFORD STREET, W.
LONDON
1892

PREFACE.

THE Council of the Library Association have arranged for the issue of a series of Handbooks on the various departments of Library work and management. Each Handbook has been entrusted to an acknowledged expert in the subject with which he will deal—and will contain the fullest and latest information that can be obtained.

Every branch of library work and method will be dealt with in detail, and the series will include a digest of Public Library Law and an account of the origin and growth of the Public Library Movement in the United Kingdom.

The comprehensive thoroughness of the one now issued is, the Editors feel, an earnest of the quality of the whole series. To mere amateurs, it may appear that it deals at needless length with matters that are perfectly familiar; but it is just this kind of thing that is really wanted by the people for whom Mr. Brown's Handbook is intended. It seems a simple matter to order a gross of chairs for a library; but only experience teaches those little points about their construction which make so much difference as regards economy and comfort.

With this Handbook in their possession, a new committee, the members of which may never have seen the inside of a public library, may furnish and equip the institution under their charge as effectively as if an experienced library manager had lent his aid.

The second issue of the series will be on "Staff," by Mr. Peter Cowell, Chief Librarian of the Liverpool Free Public Libraries.

THE EDITORS.

LONDON, *August*, 1892.

LIBRARY APPLIANCES.

THE TECHNICAL EQUIPMENT OF LIBRARIES, INCLUDING FITTINGS AND FURNITURE, RECORDS, FORMS, RECIPES, &c.

By James D. Brown, Librarian, Clerkenwell Public Library, London.

This Handbook bears some analogy to the division "miscellaneous" usually found in most library classifications. It is in some respects, perhaps, more exposed to the action of heterogeneity than even that refuge of doubt "polygraphy," as "miscellaneous" is sometimes seen disguised ; but the fact of its limits being so ill-defined gives ample scope for comprehensiveness, while affording not a little security to the compiler, should it be necessary to deprecate blame on the score of omissions or other faults. There is, unfortunately, no single comprehensive word or phrase which can be used to distinguish the special sort of library apparatus here described—"appliances" being at once too restricted or too wide, according to the standpoint adopted. Indeed there are certain bibliothecal sophists who maintain that anything is a library appliance, especially the librarian himself ; while others will have it that, when the paste-pot and scissors are included, the appliances of a library have been named. To neither extreme will this tend, but attention will be strictly confined to the machinery and implements wherewith libraries, public and other, are successfully conducted. It would be utterly impossible, were it desirable, to describe, or even mention, every variety of fitting or appliance which ingenuity and the craving for change have introduced, and the endeavour shall be accordingly to notice the more generally established apparatus, and their more important modifications. It is almost needless to point out that very many of the different methods of accomplishing the same thing, hereinafter described, result from similar causes to those which led in former times to

1

such serious political complications in the kingdom of Liliput.
There are several ways of getting into an egg, and many ways
of achieving one end in library affairs, and the very diversity of
these methods shows that thought is active and improvement
possible. As Butler has it—

> " Opiniators naturally differ
> From other men : as wooden legs are stiffer
> Than those of pliant joints, to yield and bow,
> Which way soe'er they are design'd to go ".

Hence it happens that all library appliances are subject to the
happy influences of disagreement, which, in course of time, leads
to entire changes of method and a general broadening of view.
Many of these differences arise from local conditions, or have
their existence in experiment and the modification of older ideas,
so that actual homogeneity in any series of the appliances
described in this Handbook must not be expected. It will be
sufficient if the young librarian finds enough of suggestion and
information to enable him to devise a system of library management in its minor details which shall be consistent and useful.

FITTINGS AND FURNITURE.

To some extent the arrangement of fittings and furniture will
be dealt with in the Handbook on Buildings, so that it will
only be necessary here to consider their construction, variety,
and uses.

BOOK-CASES, SHELVES, &c.

Standard cases or presses, designed for what is called the
" stack " system of arrangement, are constructed with shelves
on both sides, and are intended to stand by themselves on the
floor. They are without doors or glass fronts, and their
dimensions must be decided entirely by the requirements of
each library and the class of books they are to contain. For
ordinary lending libraries a very convenient double case with
ten shelves of books to the tier can be made about 9 feet 6 inches
wide × 8 feet 6 inches high, including cornice and plinth
× 18 inches deep—the depth of the shelves being about 9 inches,
their length 3 feet, and their thickness, as finished, not less than
$\frac{3}{4}''$ nor more than 1 inch. Such a case will hold about 1800

volumes in 8vo and 12mo sizes, and the top shelf can be reached
by a middle-sized person from a step or stool 12 inches high.
Lower cases should be provided if rapidity of service is particularly
required and there is plenty of floor space to carry the stock.
The top shelf of a case 7 feet high, including cornice and plinth,
can be reached from the floor by any one of ordinary height,
small boys and girls of course excluded. These cases are made
with middle partitions between the backs of the shelves, though

FIG. 1.*—STANDARD BOOK-CASE.

some librarians prefer a simple framework of uprights, cornice,
and plinth. For the sake of security and the necessary rigidity
a central partition ought to be included, and if this is formed of
thin ¼″ boarding, double and crossing diagonally, with a strong
iron strap between screwed tight into the outer uprights, all
tendency to bulging will be obviated, and the cases will be firm
and workmanlike. The skeleton or framework cases have to be

* For Figures 1, 3, and 7 we are indebted to Mr. Thomas Greenwood, in whose work on
Public Libraries they appear.

stayed in all directions by iron rods and squares fixed in the floor, and, when empty, look very unsightly and rickety; besides, books get pushed or tumble over on to the adjoining shelf, and the plea of ventilation, which is practically the only recommendation for this plan of construction, loses much of its

FIG. 2.*—STANDARD BOOK-CASE WITHOUT PARTITION.

weight in a lending library where most of the books are in circulation.

The shelves should have rounded edges, and ought not to exceed 3' or 3' 6" in length. If longer ones are used they must be thin, in order to be easily moved, and so these become bent in course of time, especially if heavy books are placed on them. The

* For Figures 2 and 4 we have to thank Messrs. Wako & Dean, library furnishers, London.

objection to long shelves which are very thick is simply that they are unhandy and difficult to move and waste valuable space. All shelves should be movable, and if possible interchangeable. No paint or varnish should be applied to any surface with which the books come in contact, but there is nothing to be said against polishing. Indeed, to reduce as far as possible the constant friction to which books are exposed in passing to and from their resting-places, it ought to be remembered that smooth

FIG. 3.—LEDGED WALL BOOK-CASE.

surfaces are advantageous. Few libraries can afford leather-covered shelves like those of the British Museum, but all can have smoothness and rounded edges.

Reference library cases are constructed similarly to those above described; but as folio and quarto books require storage in this department, it is necessary to make provision for them. This is usually done by making the cases with projecting bases, rising at least 3′ high, and in the enlarged space so obtained fair-sized folios and quartos can be placed. Very large volumes of plates or maps should be laid flat on shelves made to slide over hard wood runners like trays, as they frequently suffer much damage from standing upright. A special, many-shelved press should be constructed for books of this generally valuable class, and each volume should be allowed a tray for itself. If the tray is covered with leather, felt, or baize, so much the better. Wall cases, and cases arranged in bays or alcoves, are generally much more expensive than the plain standards just described, because, as they are intended for architectural effect as well as for storage, they must be ornamental, and possibly made from superior woods. The plan of arranging books round the walls has been almost entirely abandoned in modern lending libraries, but there are still many librarians and architects who prefer the bay arrangement for reference departments. The matter of arrangement is one, however, which depends largely upon the shape and lighting of rooms, means of access, and requirements of each library, and must be settled accordingly.

The question of material is very important, but of course it depends altogether upon the amount which is proposed to be spent on the fittings. It is very desirable that the cases should be made durable and handsome, as it is not pleasant to have bad workmanship and ugly fittings in a centre of "sweetness and light". For the standards previously mentioned there can be nothing better or cheaper than sound American or Baltic yellow pine, with, in reference cases, oak ledges. This wood is easily worked, wears very well, and can be effectively stained and varnished to look like richer and more expensive woods. Of course if money is no object, oak, mahogany, or walnut can be used ; but the cost of such materials usually works out to nearly double that of softer woods. Cases with heavily moulded cornices should be boarded over the top, and not left with huge empty receptacles for dust and cobwebs. This caution is tendered, because joiners very often leave the space made by the cornice vacant and exposed.

SHELF FITTINGS.

Shelf fittings for wooden book-presses are required in all modern libraries where movable shelves are almost universally used. Cases with fixed shelves are much cheaper than those fitted with one of the button or other spacing arrangements now in the market, but the serious disadvantage of having to size the books to fit the shelves disposes of any argument that can be urged on behalf of fixtures.   There are many varieties of shelf fitting designed to assist in the necessary differential spacing of shelves, from the old-fashioned, and by no means cheap, wooden ratchet and bar arrangement to the comparatively recent metal stud.   The fitting which is most often adopted in new libraries is that of Messrs. E. Tonks, of Birmingham.   It consists of metal strips, perforated at 1-inch

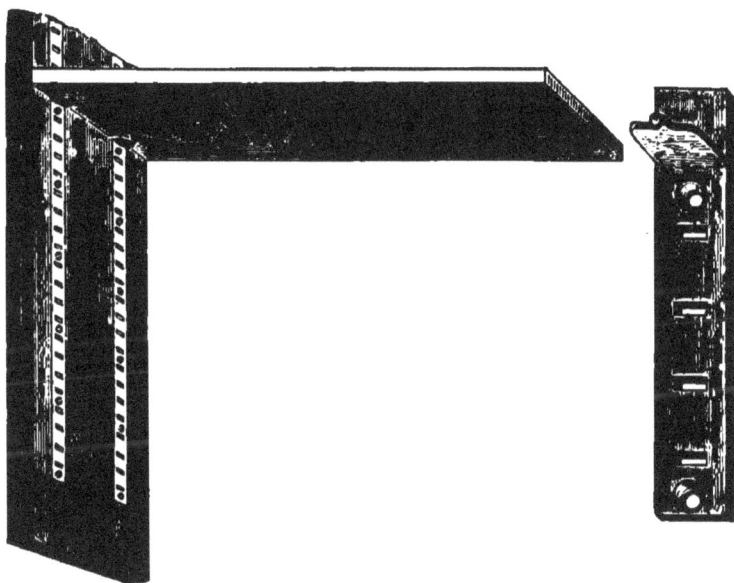

FIG. 4.—METAL SHELF FITTING.

intervals, let into the uprights of the cases and small gun-metal studs for supporting the shelves.   As is shown in the illustration, the studs fit into the perforations and support the shelves on little points which sink into the wood, and prevent tilting or sliding.   The strips should not go either to the top or bottom of the uprights, and at least two feet can be saved in every division by stopping 6 inches from both ends.   Though rather more expensive than pegs, or the studs mentioned below, it is very desirable to have Tonks' fittings, because of their superiority to all others in the matters of convenience and ease in

adjusting. Another form of stud often used is the one shaped
like this ⌐— which fits into holes drilled in the uprights
and supports the shelf on the lower rectangular part. These are
most effective in operation when let into grooves as broad as the
studs, otherwise the shelves must be cut shorter than the width of
the divisions; and in that case end spaces are caused and security
is considerably sacrificed. The peg part of this stud is very apt
in course of time, to enlarge the wooden holes, and when any
series of shelves have to be frequently moved, the result of such
enlargement is to make the studs drop out. If perforated metal
strips are used, of course the price immediately goes up, and
there is then no advantage over the Tonks' fitting. Another
form of peg for use in the same kind of round hole is that similar
in shape to the pegs used for violins, and, like them, demanding
much judicious *thumbing* before they can be properly adjusted.
There are many other kinds of shelf fitting in the market, but
none of them are so well known or useful as those just described.

IRON BOOK-CASES.

The iron book-cases manufactured by Messrs. Lucy & Co. of
Oxford are very convenient, and in buildings designed as fire-
proof, in basements, or in certain cases where much weight is
wanted to be carried, they should be useful. They can be fitted
up as continuous wall-cases, or supplied as standards holding
books on both sides. The size B, 7' 6" high × 4' 1" wide × 1' 3"
deep, will hold about 640 demy 8vo books, and the ironwork
costs £4, shelves £1 4s. Other sizes are made, and the continuous wall-shelving is charged per yard run—7 feet high, £3 3s.;
shelves of wood, 12 inches deep, 5s. each; if iron, felt covered,
4s. 6d. each. The durability of these cases is beyond question,
and the expense is not great when their security, strength, and
neatness are considered. The arrangement for spacing the shelves
is convenient and effective. The sliding iron book-cases swung
in the galleries of the British Museum, and their prototype * at
Bethnal Green Free Library, London, have been so often and so
fully described elsewhere † that it is needless to do more here than

---

* We believe the credit of this really most ingenious invention belongs to the late Dr.
Tyler, one of the founders of the Bethnal Green Free Library.—EDITORS.
  † See *Library Chronicle*, vol. iv. p. 88; Library Notes (American); and *The Library*, vol.
iii. p. 414.

to briefly refer to them.   The British Museum pattern, the invention of Mr. Jenner of the Printed Books Department, consists of a double case suspended from strong runners, which can be pushed against the permanent cases when not in use, or pulled out when books are required.   Only libraries with very wide passages between the cases could use them, and only then by greatly strengthening the ordinary wooden presses in exist- ence.*   The revolving wooden book-cases now so extensively used for office purposes, and in clubs or private libraries, can be bought for £3 and upwards.   They should not be placed for public use in ordinary libraries to which all persons have access, though there is no reason why subscription libraries and kindred institutions should not have them for the benefit of their members.

Other fittings connected with book-cases are press and shelf numbers, contents or classification frames, blinds, and shelf- edging.   The press marks used in the fixed location are sometimes painted or written in gold over the cases, but white enamelled copper tablets, with the numbers or letters painted in black or blue, are much more clear and effective.   They cost only a few pence each.   The numbering of shelves for the movable location, or their lettering for the fixed location, is usually done by means of printed labels.   These are sold in sheets, gummed and perfo- rated, and can be supplied in various sizes in consecutive series at prices ranging from 2s. 6d. per 1000 for numbers, and 1d. or 2d. each for alphabets.   Shelf numbers can also be stamped on in gold or written with paint, and brass numbers are also made for the purpose, but the cost is very great.   The little frames used for indicating the contents of a particular case or division are usually made of brass, and have their edges folded over to hold the cards.   Some are made like the sliding *carte-de-visite* frames, but the object in all is the same, namely—to carry descriptive cards referring to the contents or classification of book-cases. They are most often used in reference libraries where readers are allowed direct access to the shelves, and are commonly screwed to the uprights.   A convenient form is that used with numbered presses, and the card bears such particulars as these—

* An ingenious adaptation of this invention is suggested and described by Mr. Lymburn, Librarian of Glasgow University Library—in *The Library* for July-August, 1892.—EDITORS.

SHELF.	CASE 594.
A	Buffon's Nat. Hist.
B	Geological Rec.
C	Sach's Bot. ; Bot. Mag.
D	&c.
E	&c.
F	&c.

Others bear the book numbers, while some simply refer to the shelf contents as part of a particular scheme of classification, viz.:—

941·1 Northern Scotland.

To keep these contents-cards clean it is usual to cover them with little squares of glass.

Glazed book-cases are not recommended, wire-work being much better in cases where it is necessary to have locked doors. The mesh of the wire-work should be as fine as possible, because valuable bindings are sometimes nail-marked and scratched by inquisitive persons poking through at the books. It is only in very special circumstances that locked presses are required, such as when they are placed in a public reading-room or in a passage, and though glazed book-cases are a tradition among house furnishers, no librarian will have them if it can possibly be avoided. Their preservative value is very questionable, and books do very well in the open, while there can be no two opinions as to their being a source of considerable trouble. Blinds concealed in the cornices of book-cases are sometimes used, their object being to protect the books from dust during the night, but they do not seem to be wanted in public libraries. In regard to the various shelf-edgings seen in libraries, leather is only ornamental, certainly not durable ; while scalloped cloth, though much more effective, may also be dispensed with.

COUNTERS, CUPBOARDS, &c.

To the practical librarian a good counter is a source of perennial joy. It is not only the theatre of war, and the centre to which every piece of work undertaken by the library converges, but it is a barrier over which are passed most of the suggestions and criticisms which lead to good work, and from which can be gleaned the best idea of the business accomplished. For these reasons alone a first-class counter is very desirable. As in every other branch of library management, local circumstances must govern the size and shape of the counter to be provided. Lending libraries using indicators require a different kind of counter than those which use ledgers or card-charging systems, and reference libraries must have them according to the plan of arrangement followed for the books. A lending library counter where no indicator is used need not be a very formidable affair, but it ought to afford accommodation for at least six persons standing abreast, and have space for a screened desk and a flap giving access to the public side. On the staff side should be plenty of shelves, cupboards, and drawers, and it may be found desirable to place in it a locked till also for the safe-keeping of money received for fines, catalogues, &c. All counter-tops should project several inches beyond the front to keep back the damage-working toes of the public, and on the staff side a space of at least 3 inches should be left under the pot-board. A height of 3 feet and a width of 2 feet will be found convenient dimensions for reference and non-indicator lending library counters. Where indicators are used a width of 18 inches and a height of 30 or 32 inches will be found best. If the counter is made too high and wide neither readers nor assistants can conveniently see or reach the top numbers. As regards length, everything will depend on the indicator used and the size of the library. An idea of the comparative size of some indicators may be got from the following table :—

Counter space required for 12,000 numbers	... Cotgreave 15 feet.
" " "	... Elliot (small) 16 feet.
" " "	... Duplex (small) 22 feet.
" " "	... " (full) 32 feet.
" " "	... Elliot (full) 36 feet.

Allowing 12 feet of counter space for service of readers, 2 feet for desk space, and 2 feet for flap, a Cotgreave indicator for 12,000 numbers would mean a counter 31 feet long, a small Elliot 32 feet, a small Duplex 38 feet, a full Duplex 48 feet, and a full Elliot 52 feet. For double the quantity of numbers the smallest indicator would require a counter 46 feet long, and the largest one 88 feet.

These are important points to bear in mind when planning the counter; though it must be said generally that, in nearly every instance where a Library Committee has proceeded with the fitting of a new building before appointing a librarian, they are over-looked, because the architect invariably provides a counter about 6 feet long, 3 feet wide, and 3 feet high, with a carved front of surpassing excellence! What has been already said respecting materials applies with equal force to this class of fitting; but it should be added that a good hard-wood counter will likely last for ever. Some librarians who use card catalogues prefer to keep them in drawers opening to the public side of the reference library counter. This point is worth remembering in connection with the fitting of the reference department.

In addition to the store cupboards provided behind the counters there should be plenty of wall or other presses fixed in convenient places for holding stationery, supplies of forms, &c. Locked store presses are also useful; and every large library should have a key-press, in which should be hung every public key belonging to the building, properly numbered and labelled to correspond with a list pasted inside the press itself. These useful little cabinets are infinitely superior to the caretaker's pocket, and much inconvenience is avoided by their use. Desks for the staff use should be made with a beading all round the top and at bottom of slope to prevent papers, pens, and ink from falling or being pushed over. Superintendents' desks should be made large, and to stand on a double pedestal of drawers, so that they may be high enough for useful oversight and capacious enough for stationery or other supplies. There is an admirable specimen of a superintendent's desk in the Mitchell Library, Glasgow.

FURNITURE.

Tables for reading or writing at are best made in the form of a double desk,  which gives readers the most convenience, and affords an effective but unobtrusive means of mutual oversight. The framing and rails should be as shallow as possible, so as not to interfere with the comfort of readers, and elaborately turned or carved legs should be avoided, because certain

to harbour dust, and likely to form resting-places for feet.   Tables
with flat tops resting on central pedestals, and without side rails,
are very useful in general reading-rooms, the free leg space being
a decided advantage.   Long tables are not recommended, nor are
narrow ones which accommodate readers on one side only.   The

FIG. 5.

FIG. 6.

Figures 5, 6, and 8 are inserted by kind permission of Messrs. Hammer & Co.,
library furnishers, London.

former are obstructive, and the latter are neither economical as
regards the seating of readers, nor of much use for the necessary
mutual oversight which ought to be promoted among the public.
Very good dimensions for reading-room tables are 8 to 10 feet
long by 3 to 3 feet 6 inches wide by 2 feet 6 inches high.

But the librarian who wishes to consult the varying requirements of his readers will have his tables made different heights —some 29, some 30, and some 32 inches high. Whatever materials may be used for the framing and legs of tables, let the tops be hard-wood, like American or English oak, mahogany, or walnut. Teak is handsome and very durable, but its cost is much more than the better known woods. Yellow pine is too soft and looks common, and should not be used for tops unless the most rigid economy is absolutely necessary. Heavy tables, like those used in clubs, are not recommended. Ink wells, if provided at all, should be let in flush with the tops of the desk tables, and ought to have sliding brass covers, with thumb-notches for moving instead of knobs. Two common forms of library tables are shown in the annexed illustrations. The one on pedestals need not have such large brackets, and the ends can easily be allowed to project at least 18 inches from the pedestals in order to admit of readers sitting at them. In connection with tables there are various kinds of reading slopes made for large books, of which those with movable supporters working in a ratcheted base are the most useful. But there are endless varieties of such reading desks or stands in existence, and some invalid-appliance makers manufacture many different kinds.

PERIODICAL RACKS.

Librarians are not unanimous as regards the treatment of the current numbers of periodicals. Some maintain that they should be spread all over the tables of the reading-room in any order, to ensure that all shall receive plenty of attention at the *hands* of readers, whether they are wanted or not for perusal. Others hold the opinion that the periodicals in covers should be spread over the tables, but in some recognised order, alphabetical or otherwise. Yet another section will have it that this spreading should be accompanied by fixing, and that each cover should be fastened in its place on the table. Finally, many think that the magazines, &c., should be kept off the tables entirely, and be arranged in racks where they will be accessible without littering the room, and at the same time serve as a sort of indicator to periodicals which are in or out of use. For the unfixed alphabetical arrangement several appliances have been introduced.   At Manchester the periodicals are arranged on raised desks along the middle of the tables.   In the Mitchell Library, Glasgow, each table is surmounted by a platform raised on brackets which carries the magazine covers, without altogether obstructing the reader's view of the room and his neighbours.   Each periodical is given a certain place on the elevated carriers, and this is indicated to the reader by a label fixed on the rail behind the cover.   On the cover itself is stamped the name of the periodical and its table number.   Each table has a list of the periodicals belonging to it shown in a glazed tablet at the outer end of the platform support.   Wolverhampton and St. Martin's, London, furnish very good examples of the fixed arrangement.   In the former library each periodical is fastened to its table by a rod, and has appropriated to it a chair, so that removal and disarrangement cannot occur.   In the latter those located in the newsroom are fastened on stands where chairs cannot be used, and the arrangement is more economical as regards space than at Wolverhampton.   The periodicals in the magazine room are fixed by cords to the centre of the table and signboards indicate the location of each periodical.   This seems to be the best solution of the difficulty after all.   Every periodical in this library is fixed, more or less, and it is therefore easy to find out if a periodical is in use.

The rack system has many advocates, and can be seen both in libraries and clubs in quite a variety of styles.   At the London Institution there is an arrangement of rails and narrow beaded shelves on the wall, which holds a large number of periodicals not in covers, and seems to work very well.   The rails are fastened horizontally about two inches from the walls at a distance above the small shelf sufficient to hold and keep upright the periodicals proposed to be placed on it, and a small label bearing a title being fixed on the rail, the corresponding periodical is simply dropped behind it on to the shelf, and so remains located.   A similar style of rail-rack has been introduced for time-tables, &c., in several libraries, and has been found very useful.   Another style of periodical-rack is that invented by Mr. Alfred Cotgreave, whereby periodicals are displayed on two sides of a large board, and secured in their places by means of clips.   The same inventor has also an arrangement similar to that described as in the London Institution for magazines in

covers. The ordinary clip-rack used largely by newsvendors
has been often introduced in libraries where floor space was not
available, and is very convenient for keeping in order the shoals
of presented periodicals, which live and die like mushrooms, and
scarcely ever justify the expense of a cover. An improvement on
the usual perpendicular wall-rack just mentioned is that used in
the National Liberal Club, London, which revolves on a stand,
and can be made to hold two or three dozen periodicals or
newspapers, according to dimensions.

The racks just mentioned are all designed to hold periodicals
without covers, but there are several kinds in existence for

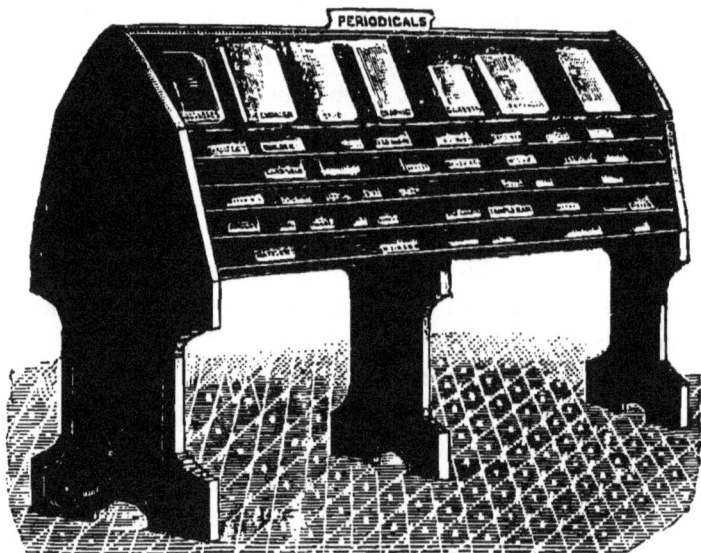

FIG. 7.—PERIODICAL RACK.

holding them in their covers. Among such are the table supports,
in metal and wood, on the same principle as shelf book-holders,
in which the magazines lie in their cases on their fore-edges, and
are distinguished by having the titles lettered along the back or
otherwise. Probably the best of all the racks devised for periodicals in their cases is that on the system of overlapping sloping
shelves, shown in the illustration. The idea of this rack is
simply that the covers should lie on the shelves with only the
title exposed. They are retained in place by a beading just deep
enough to afford a catch for one cover, and so avoid the chance

of their being hidden by another periodical laid above. These racks can also be made single to stand against the wall if floor space is not available. Oak, walnut, and mahogany are the best woods to use, but pitch or ordinary yellow pine may also be used.

NEWSPAPER STANDS.

The day has not yet come when octavo-sized newspapers will obviate the necessity for expensive and obstructive stands on which the day's news is spread in the manner least conducive to the comfort of readers. The man who runs

Fig. 8.—NEWSPAPER STAND.

and reads has no necessity for much study, while he who stands and reads does so with the consciousness that at any moment he may be elbowed from his studies by impatient news-seekers, and be subjected to the added discomfort of being made a leaning pillar for half-a-dozen persons to embrace. Meanwhile it is necessary to provide convenient reading desks for the broadsheets which are issued. It is cheaper to have double stands, holding four spread papers, than single ones, holding only two, though there is certainly less comfort to readers with the larger size. The illustration shows a single

2

stand, but it should be remembered that the design can be made much heavier and richer. The dimensions should be for double stands 7' 6" long, 2' 6" high for slope, and about 3' from floor to bottom of slope. Single ones should be 4' long, with the other measurements as before. Half-stands for going against the wall have only the slope to the front, and are generally made in long lengths to cover the whole side of a room. The slope should not in any case be made either too steep or too great--the former always causing the papers to droop, and the latter placing the upper parts beyond the sight of short persons. Before adopting any type of stand, it is advisable to visit a few other libraries and examine their fittings. It is so much easier to judge what is liked best by actual examination. Fittings for holding the newspapers in their places are generally made of wood or brass, and there are many different kinds in use. The wooden ones usually consist of a narrow oak bar, fitted with spikes to keep the paper up, hinged at top and secured at bottom of the slope by a staple and padlock, or simply by a button. The brass ones include some patented fittings, such as Cummings', made by Messrs. Denison of Leeds, and Hills', invented by the library superintendent of Bridgeport, Connecticut. The former is a rod working n an eccentric bed, and is turned with a key to tighten or loosen it ; the latter works on a revolving pivot secured in the middle of the desk, and is intended more particularly for illustrated periodicals, like the *Graphic*, &c., which require turning about to suit the pictures. The " Burgoyne " spring rod made by the North of England School Furnishing Co., Darlington and London, is very effective, neat, and comparatively inexpensive. It is secured by a catch, which requires a key to open it, but it is simply snapped down over the paper when changes are made. Other varieties of brass holders are those secured by ordinary locks or strong thumb-screws. In cases where the rods have no spikes (which are not recommended) or buttons, or which do not lie in grooves, it is advisable to have on them two stout rubber rings, which will keep the papers firmly pressed in their places, and so prevent slipping. A half-inch beading along the bottom of the slope is sometimes useful in preventing doubling down and slipping. The names of the papers may be either gilded or painted on the title-board, or they may be done in black or blue letters on white enamelled title-pieces and screwed to the head board. These latter are very cheap, durable, and clear. Some librarians prefer movable titles ; and in this case grooved holders or brass frames must be provided to hold the names, which can be printed on stiff cards, or painted on wood or bone tablets. The brass rail at the foot of the slope, shown in the illustration, is meant to prevent readers from leaning on the papers with their arms. By some librarians it is thought quite unnecessary, by others it is considered essential; but it is really a matter for the decision of every individual librarian.

CHAIRS AND MISCELLANEOUS MATTERS.

The chairs made in Buckinghamshire and Oxfordshire are the best and cheapest in the market, and more satisfaction will result from orders placed direct with the makers than from purchasing at an ordinary furniture dealer's. It is better to have small chairs made with the back and back legs all in one piece, thus, ⊨ rather than with legs and back rails all separately glued into the seat like this, ⊨ The reason is of course that by the former plan of construction greater strength is obtained, and future trouble in the way of repairs will be largely obviated. Avoid showy chairs, and everything that smacks of the cheap furniture market. It will strengthen the chairs to have hat rails as well as ordinary side rails, and be a convenience to readers as well. They should cross from the bottom side rail, thus, ⊨ Arm-chairs should be provided at discretion. In magazine rooms where there is a rack, tables can be largely dispensed with if arm-chairs are used. If neither wood-block flooring nor linoleum is used, the chairs may with great advantage be shod with round pieces of sole leather screwed through a slightly sunk hole to the ends of the legs. These deaden the noise of moving greatly, and are more durable than india-rubber. Two or three dozen of chairs more than are actually required should be ordered. Umbrella stands are best patronised when attached to the tables, like ordinary pew ones.

An umbrella stand close to the door is such an obvious temptation to the thief that careful readers never use them on any consideration. Of rails for fixing to the tables there are many kinds, but probably the hinged pew variety, plain rail, or rubber wheel, all with water-pans, will serve most purposes. Many libraries make no provision at all either of hat rails or umbrella stands, for the simple reason that 50% of the readers do not enter to stay, while 99% never remove their hats. In proprietary libraries everything is different, and an approach to comforts of the sort indicated must be made. The standard hat rack and umbrella stand combined, like that used in clubs, schools, the House of Commons, &c., is the best for such institutions.

Show-cases ought to be well made by one of the special firms who make this class of fitting. Glass sides and sliding trays, with hinged and *locked* backs, are essential. For museum purposes all sorts of special cases are required, and the only way to find out what is best is to visit one or two good museums for the purpose.

TECHNICAL APPLIANCES.

CHARGING SYSTEMS AND INDICATORS.—The charging of books includes every operation connected with the means taken to record issues and returns, whether in lending or reference libraries. Although the word "charging" refers mainly to the actual entry or booking of an issue to the account of a borrower, it has been understood in recent years to mean the whole process of counter work in circulating libraries. It is necessary to make this explanation at the outset, as many young librarians understand the meaning of the word differently. For example, one bright young man on being asked what was the system of "charging" pursued in his library responded: "Oh! just a penny for the ticket!" And another equally intelligent assistant replied to the same question: "We don't charge anything unless you keep books more than the *proscribed* time!" Before proceeding to describe some of the existing systems it may be wise to impress on assistants in libraries the advisability of trying to think for themselves in this matter. There is nothing more discouraging than to find young librarians slavishly following the methods bequeathed by their predecessors, because in no sphere of public work is there a larger field for substantial improvement, or less reason to suppose that readers are as easily satisfied as they were thirty years ago. The truth is that every library method is more or less imperfect in matters of detail, and there are numerous directions in which little improvements tending to greater homogeneity and accuracy can be effected. It is all very well, and likewise easy, to sit at the feet of some bibliothecal Gameliel, treasuring his dicta as incontrovertible, and at the same time assuming that the public is utterly indifferent to efficiency and simplicity of system. But it ought to be seriously considered that everything changes, and that the public knowledge of all that relates to their welfare increases every day ; so that the believer in a *dolce far niente* policy must be prepared for much adverse· criticism, and possibly for improvements being effected in his despite, which is very unpleasant. In libraries conducted for profit, everything likely to lead to extension of business, or to the increased convenience of the public, is at once adopted, and it is this sort of generous flexibility which ought to be more largely imported into public library management. A suitable reverence for the good work accomplished in the past should be no obstacle to improvement and enlargement of ideas in the future.

LEDGERS.

The present state of the question of charging turns largely on the respective merits of indicator and non-indicator systems, or, in other words, whether the burden of ascertaining if books are *in* or *out* should be placed on readers or the staff. There is much to be said on both sides, and reason to suppose that the final solution lies with neither. The non-indicator systems come first as a matter of seniority. The advantages of all ledger and card-charging systems are claimed to be that readers are admitted directly to the benefit of intercourse with the staff; that they are saved the trouble of discovering if the numbers they want are in ; that they are in very many cases better served, because more accustomed to explain their wants ; that less counter space is required ; that the initial expense of an indicator is saved ; and, finally, that with a good staff borrowers can be more quickly attended to. Some of these statements may be called in question, but they represent the views of librarians

who have tried both systems. From the readers' point of view
there can hardly be a doubt but that the least troublesome system
is the most acceptable ; and it is only fair to the non-indicator
systems to assert that they *are* the least troublesome to borrowers. The original method of charging, still used in many
libraries, consisted in making entries of all issues in a day-book
ruled to show the following particulars :—

DATE OF ISSUE.

1	2	3	4	5	6	7	8	9
Pro-gressive No.	Title of Book.	Class Letter.	No.	Vols.	Date of Return.	Name of Borrower.	No. of Card.	Fines.
1								
2								
3								

But after a time certain economies were introduced, columns 2, 7,
and 9 being omitted, and day-books in this later form, perhaps
with the arrangement slightly altered, are in common use now.
Of course it is plain that a book on issue was entered in the first
vacant line of the day-book, and the progressive number, borrower's number, and date were carried on to its label. On
return, the particulars on the label pointed out the day and
issue number, and the book was duly marked off. It will at
once be seen that this form of ledger only shows what books are
out, but cannot readily show the whereabouts of any particular
volume without some trouble. As to what book any reader has
is another question which cannot be answered without much
waste of time. A third disadvantage is that as borrowers
retain their tickets there is very little to prevent unscrupulous
persons from having more books out at one time than they should.
A fourth weakness of this ledger is that time is consumed in
marking off, and books are not available for re-issue until they are
marked off. For various reasons some librarians prefer a system
of charging direct to each borrower instead of journalising the
day's operations as above described. These records were at one
time kept in ledgers, each borrower being apportioned a page or

so, headed with full particulars of his name, address, guarantor, date of the expiry of his borrowing right, &c. These ledgers were ruled to show date of issue, number of book, and date of return, and an index had to be consulted at every entry. Now-a-days this style of ledger is kept on cards arranged alphabetically or numerically, and is much easier to work. Subscription and commercial circulating libraries use the system extensively. The main difficulty with this system was to find out who had a particular book; and "overdues" were hard to discover, and much time was consumed in the process. To some extent both these defects could be remedied by keeping the borrowers' cards and arranging them in dated trays, so that as books were returned and the cards gradually weeded out from the different days of issue, a deposit of overdue borrowers' cards pointing to their books would result. Another form of ledger is just the reverse of the last, the reader being charged to the book instead of the book to the reader. This is a specimen :—

K 5942.   WOOD—EAST LYNNE.

Date of Issue.	Borrowers' No.	Date of Return.	Date of Issue.	Borrowers' No.	Date of Return.
4 May	395	18 May			
6 June	3421				

Every book has a page or more, according to popularity, and there can hardly be a doubt of its superiority to the personal ledger, because the question of a book's whereabouts is more often raised than what book a given reader has. Dates of issue and return are stamped, and all books are available for issue on return. The borrowers' cards, if kept in dated trays as above, show at once "overdues" and who have books out. But the "overdues" can be ascertained also by periodical examination of the ledger. In this system book ledgers are as handy as cards. In both of the ledger systems above described classified day sheets for statistical purposes are used. They are generally ruled thus :—

DATE.

A	B	C	D	E	F

and the issues are recorded by means of strokes or other figures. At one time it was considered an ingenious arrangement to have a series of boxes lettered according to classes, with locked doors and apertures at the top, in which a pea could be dropped for every issue in any class ; but this seems to have been now completely abandoned. Certainly neither the sheet-stroking nor pea-dropping method of getting at the number of daily issues can be recommended, because in both cases the account is at the mercy of assistants, who may either neglect to make such charges, or register some dozen issues at a time to account for intervals spent in idling. An application slip is the best solution of the difficulty. This can either be filled up by the assistants or the borrowers. In certain libraries these slips are of some permanence, being made of stout paper in long narrow strips, on which borrowers enter their ticket-numbers and the numbers and classes of the books they would like. The assistant stamps the current date against the book had out, and the slips, after the statistics are compiled from them, are sorted in order of borrowers' numbers and placed in dated trays. Of course when the borrower returns the book, his list is looked out, and the name of the returned book heavily cancelled and another work procured as before. There are various kinds of ticket-books issued for this purpose, some with counterfoils and detachable cheques, and others with similar perforated slips and ruled columns for lists of books wanted to read. Messrs. Lupton & Co. of Birmingham, Mr. Ridal of Rotherham Free Library, and Messrs. Waterston & Sons, stationers, Edinburgh, all issue different varieties of call-books, or lists of wants. Some libraries provide slips of paper, on which the assistant jots down the book-number after the borrower hands it in with his ticket-number written in thus :—

Ticket.	Book.
5963	C 431

These are simply filed at the moment of service, and become the basis of the statistical entry for each day's operations. Such slips save the loss of time which often arises when careful entries have to be made on day-sheets or books, and there can be no question as to their greater accuracy. These are the main points in connection with the most-used class of day-books and ledgers.

CARD-CHARGING SYSTEMS.

Somewhat akin to the ledger systems are the various card- and pocket-charging methods which work without the intervention of an indicator. There are several of such systems in existence both in Britain and the United States, most of them having features in common, but all distinguished by differences on points of detail. At Bradford a pocket system has long been in use. It is worked as follows : Every book has attached to one of the inner sides of its boards a linen pocket, with a table of months for dating, and an abstract of the lending rules. Within this pocket is a card on which are the number and class of the book, its title and author. To each reader is issued on joining a cloth-covered card and a pocket made of linen, having on one side the borrower's number, name, address, &c., and on the other side a calendar. The pockets are kept in numerical order at the library, and the readers retain their cards. When a borrower wishes a book, he hands in a list of numbers and his card to the assistant, who procures the first book he finds in. He next selects from the numerical series of pockets the one bearing the reader's number. The title card is then removed from the book and placed in the reader's numbered pocket, and the date is written in the date column of the book pocket. This completes the process at the time of service. At night the day's issues are classified and arranged in the order of the book numbers, after the statistics are made up and noted in the sheet ruled for the purpose, and are then placed in a box bearing the date of issue.

When a book is returned the assistant turns up its date of issue, proceeds to the box of that date, and removes the title card, which he replaces in the book. The borrower's pocket is then restored to its place among its fellows. The advantages of this plan are greater rapidity of service as compared with the ledger systems, and a mechanical weeding out of overdues somewhat similar to what is obtained by the "Duplex" indicator system described further on. Its disadvantages are the absence of permanent record, and the danger which exists of title cards getting into the wrong pockets.

A system on somewhat similar lines is worked at Liverpool and Chelsea, the difference being that in these libraries a record is made of the issues of books. It has the additional merit of being something in the nature of a compromise between a ledger and an indicator system, so that to many it will recommend itself on these grounds alone. The Cotgreave indicator is in this system used for fiction and juvenile books only, and as the records of issues are made on cards, the indicator is simply used to show books *out* and *in.* Mr. George Parr, of the London Institution, is the inventor of an admirable card-ledger, and though it has been in use for a number of years its merits do not seem to be either recognised or widely known. The main feature of this system, which was described at the Manchester meeting of the L.A.U.K. in 1879, is a fixed alphabetical series of borrowers' names on cards, behind which other cards descriptive of books issued are placed. The system is worked as follows: Every book has a pocket inside the board somewhat similar to that used at Bradford and Chelsea, in which is a card bearing the title and number of the book. When the book is issued the card is simply withdrawn and placed, with a coloured card to show the date, behind the borrower's card in the register. When it is returned the title card is simply withdrawn from behind the borrower's card, replaced in the book, and the transaction is complete. This is the brief explanation of its working, but Mr. Parr has introduced many refinements and devices whereby almost any question that can be raised as regards who has a book, when it was issued, and what book a given person has, can be answered with very little labour. This is accomplished by means of an ingenious system of projecting guides on the cards, together with different colours for each 1000 members, and with these aids a ready means is afforded of accurately finding the location in the card-ledger of any given book or borrower. As regards its application to a popular public library, the absence of a permanent record would in most cases be deemed objectionable, but there seems no reason why, with certain modifications, it could not be adapted to the smaller libraries, where neither pocket systems nor indicators are in use. This very ingenious and admirable system suggests what seems in theory a workable plan for any library up to 10,000 volumes. Instead of making a fixed alphabet of borrowers, as in Mr. Parr's model, a series of cards might be prepared, one for each book in the library, in numerical order, distributed in hundreds and tens, shown by projections to facilitate finding. A label would be placed in each book, ruled to take the borrower's number and date of issue, and a borrower's card like that used for Mr. Elliot's indicator, ruled to take the book numbers only. When a book is asked for, all that the assistant has to do is to write its number in the borrower's card, the number of the borrower's card and the date on the book label, and then to issue the book, having left the borrower's card in the register. The period of issue could be indicated by differently coloured cards to meet the overdue question, and a simple day-sheet ruled for class letters and numbers of books issued would serve for statistical purposes. The register of book-numbers could be used as an indicator by the staff in many cases, and such a plan would be as easily worked, as economical, and as accurate as most of the charging systems in use in small libraries.

There are many other card-charging systems in use, but most of them are worked only in the United States. A large number of British libraries, especially those established under the " Public Libraries Acts," use one or other of the various indicators which have been introduced since 1870, and it now becomes necessary to describe some of these.

INDICATORS.

The first indicator of any practical use was that invented by Mr. John Elliot, of Wolverhampton, in 1870. Previous to that date various make-shift contrivances had been used to aid the staff in finding what books were in or out without

the trouble of actually going to the shelves, chief among which
was a board drilled with numbered holes to receive pegs when
the books represented by the numbers were out. Elliot's indicator is a large framework of wood, divided, as shown in the
engraving, into ten divisions by wooden uprights, on which are
fastened printed columns of numbers 1 to 100, 101 to 200, &c.,
representing volumes in the library. Between each number, in
the spaces between the uprights, are fastened small tin slides,

FIG. 9.*—ELLIOT'S INDICATOR.

forming a complete series of tiny shelves for the reception of
borrowers' tickets, which are placed against the numbers of the
books taken out. The numbers are placed on both sides of the
indicator, which is put on the counter, with one side glazed to
face the borrowers. Its working is simple: Every borrower
receives on joining a ticket in the shape of a book, having spaces

* For Figures 9, 11, 13, 14, and 17 we are indebted to Mr. Greenwood's work on Public
Libraries.

ruled to show the numbers of books and dates of issue, with the ends coloured red and green. On looking at the indicator the borrower sees so many vacant spaces opposite numbers, and so many occupied by cards, and if the number he wishes is shown blank he knows it is *in* and may be applied for. He accordingly does so, and the assistant procures the book, writes in the borrower's card the number and date of issue, and on the issue-label of the book the reader's ticket-number and date. When the book is returned the assistant simply removes the borrower's card from the space and returns it, and the transaction is complete. A day-sheet is commonly used for noting the number of issues; but, of course, application forms can also be used. The coloured ends of the borrowers' tickets are used to show over-due books, red being turned outwards one fortnight, or what-ever the time allowed may be, and green the next. Towards the end of the second period the indicator is searched for the first colour, and the "overdues" noted. The main defect of the Elliot indicator lies in the danger which exists of readers' tickets being placed in the wrong spaces, when they are practically lost.

The "Cotgreave" indicator, invented by Mr. Alfred Cotgreave, now librarian of West Ham, London, differs from the Elliot in principle and appearance, and is more economical in the space required. It consists of an iron frame, divided into columns of 100 by means of wooden uprights and tin slides; but has numbered blank books in every space, instead of an alternation of numbered uprights and spaces. Into each space is fitted a movable metal case, cloth-covered, containing a miniature ledger ruled to carry a record of borrowers' numbers and dates of issue. These cases are turned up at each end, thus {_____}, and the book-number appears at one end on a red ground and at the other on a blue ground.

The blue end is shown to the public to indicate books *in*, and the red end to indicate books *out*. The ordinary method of working it is as follows: The borrower, having found the number of the book wanted indicated *in* (blue), asks for it by number at the counter, and hands over his ticket. The assistant, having procured the book, next withdraws the indicator-book and enters in the first blank space the reader's ticket-number and the date, reverses the little ledger to show the number *out*, and leaves in it the borrower's card; stamps or writes the date on the issue-label of the book, and gives it to the reader. On return the indicator number is simply turned round, and the borrower receives back his card. "Overdues" can be shown by means of coloured clips, or by having the borrowers' cards shaped or coloured, and issues are recorded on day-sheets, or by means of application forms. There are, however, endless ways of working both the Elliot and Cot-

FIG. 10.*—COTGREAVE'S INDICATOR.

greave indicators, though there is only space to describe the most elementary forms. Like every other department of library work, the working of an indicator-charging system will bear careful thought, and leave room for original developments. The " Duplex" indicator, invented by Mr. A. W. Robertson, librarian of

* We are obliged to Messrs. Wake & Dean for the Figures Nos. 10, 15 and 16.

Aberdeen, has several novel features which call for attention. A full-sized Duplex indicator occupies 5 ft. 4 in. of counter space for every 2000 numbers, while a smaller pattern for a similar number occupies 3 ft. 8 in. of counter space, both being 4 ft. high, and is a frame fitted with slides in the manner of the Cotgreave and Elliot indicators. It is also a catalogue, and the numbers and titles of ' books are given on the blocks which fit into numbered spaces. Each block has a removable and reversible sheet for carrying a record consisting of borrower's number, number in ticket-register, and date of issue. The borrowers' cards are made of wood, and also bear a removable slip for noting the numbers of books read. When a book is asked for the assistant proceeds first to the indicator and removes the block, which bears on its surface the location marks and accession number of the book, and on one end the number and title of the book; the other being coloured red to indicate *out*, but also bearing the number. He then carries the reader's number on to the block, and having got and issued the book, leaves the block and card on a tray. This is all that is done at the moment of issue, and it is simple enough, all the registration being postponed till another time. The assistant who does this takes a tray of blocks and cards and sits down in front of the ticket-register, which is a frame divided into compartments, consecutively numbered up to five hundred or more, and bearing the date of issue. He then selects a card and block, carries the book-number on to the borrower's card, and the number of the first vacant ticket-register compartment, with the date, on to the book block, and leaves the borrower's card in the register. Probably the statistical returns will also be made up at this time. The blocks are then placed reversed in the indicator, and so are shown out to the public. When a book is returned, the assistant proceeds to the indicator to turn the block, and while doing so notes the date and register number, and then removes and returns the borrower's card. By this process the ticket-register is gradually weeded, till on the expiry of the period during which books can be kept without fine, all tickets remaining are removed to the overdue register, which bears the same date, and are placed in its compartments according to the order of the ticket-register. A slip bearing those numbers is pinned down the side of the overdue register so that defaulters can easily be found.

These are the principal points in the three best indicators yet

invented, and it only remains to note their differences. The
Elliot indicator system makes the charge to the borrower, and
preserves no permanent record of book issues apart from the
label in the book itself. The Cotgreave system charges the
borrower to the book, and *does* keep a permanent record of the
issues. The "Duplex" system shows who has had a certain
book, what books a certain reader has had, in addition to a
record on the book itself similar to that kept with the Elliot and
Cotgreave systems, but only in a temporary manner. So far as
permanency of record is concerned the Cotgreave is the only indicator which keeps this in itself. The reading done by borrowers
is not shown in a satisfactory manner by any of the three systems,
as worked in their elementary stages, and the Elliot and Duplex
records are only available when the readers' tickets are in the
library *and their places known*. Much difference of opinion
exists among librarians as regards the necessity for a double
entry charging system, many experienced men holding that a
simple record of the issues of a book is all that is required.
Others are equally positive that a separate record of a borrower's
reading is only a logical outcome of the spirit of public library
work, which aims at preserving, as well as compiling, full information touching public use and requirements. In this view the
writer agrees, and strongly recommends every young librarian to
avoid the slipshod, and go in heart and soul for thoroughness.
A simple double record of borrowers' reading and books read,
which will give as little trouble to the public as possible, is much
required, and will repay the attention bestowed on it by the
young librarian. Where application slips are used, which give
book- and borrower-numbers, it is a simple matter compiling a
daily record of the reading done by each borrower. At several
libraries where Cotgreave's indicator is used, it is done by the
process of pencilling the number of the book taken out on to a
card bearing the reader's number. These cards form a numerical
register of borrowers, and are posted up from the application
forms.

Before leaving the subject of charging systems let it again be
strongly urged that no system of charging should be adopted
without a careful thinking-out of the whole question ; giving due
consideration of the matters before raised, at counters (p. 10)
and above, touching space and public convenience in the use of

indicators. Though it is claimed for the indicator that it reduces friction between assistant and public, facilitates service, and secures impartiality, it should be remembered that it is expensive; occupies much space; abolishes most of the helpful relations between readers and staff; quickens service only to the staff; and after all is not infallible in its working, especially when used without any kind of cross-check such as is afforded by application forms and separate records of issues to borrowers.

Reference library charging is usually accomplished by placing the reader's application in the place vacated by the book asked for, and removing and signing it on return. In some libraries these slips are kept for statistical purposes; in others they are returned to the reader as a sort of receipt; and in others, again, the form has a detachable portion which is used for the same purpose. In some libraries two different colours of slips are used to facilitate the examination of the shelves on the morning after the issues.

CATALOGUING APPARATUS.

In this section will be noticed only catalogue-holders, or accession-frames, together with any mechanical apparatus used in the production of catalogues. Cabinets for holding card-catalogues are made in a variety of styles, some being drawers fitted into the fronts of counters, and others being independent stands of drawers. The usual style of cabinet at present used provides for the cards being strung through oval or rounded holes on to brass rods, which are fixed, to prevent readers from removing them and so upsetting the order of the cards. The drawers themselves are made to pull out only as far as necessary, in order to prevent careless users from pulling them out altogether and working destruction to both fittings and arrangement. The construction of these cabinets should only be entrusted to skilled workmen, and only oak, walnut, or other hard woods should be used. As every librarian has his or her own opinion as to how such cabinets should be made and their contents safeguarded, it will be best to refer inquirers to examples of such catalogues in actual work, in different styles, at Liverpool, Newcastle-on-Tyne, Nottingham ; the Royal College of Surgeons, Guildhall, Battersea, St. Martin-in-the-Fields, and Clerkenwell, London, and elsewhere. A special cabinet is made by Messrs. Stone of Banbury, Oxon., but its safeguards require to be improved. A half-falling front locked on to the rod which secures the cards is a very simple and effective plan of keeping order in isolated cabinets. In cases where the backs of the drawers are get-at-able from the staff side of the counter, even more simple methods of securing the cards, while giving every facility in the way of making additions, can be adopted. Projecting guides to show in index style the whereabouts of particular parts of the alphabet should be made either of tin or linen-mounted cards. Tin lasts best, although the lettering sometimes rubs off. Nothing will satisfy a librarian, who has a card-catalogue in contemplation, so much as the comparison of the kinds adopted in different libraries. The chief objection to card cabinets or drawers is the insurmountable one of limitation to public use being fixed by the number of drawers or cabinets. With drawers in a counter front one consulter monopolises one drawer, while with tiers of three or four drawers in cabinet form never more than two persons can use it with any comfort. The exposure of only one title at a time is another serious drawback, while the peculiar daintiness of touch requisite for the proper manipulation of the cards makes the use of the catalogue a labour and a perplexity to working people with hardened finger-tips. We think it likely, therefore, that catalogues in a large series of handy guard-books, or in volumes or boxes provided with an arrangement for inserting slips of additions, will in the future come to be recognised as that best adapted for general use. A card-catalogue for staff use ought in any case to be kept, either in boxes or covered trays. Another catalogue appliance is the accession-frame, or device for making public all recent additions to the library. Of these there are several, but we need only mention a few as typical of the rest. At some libraries a glazed case with shelves is placed on the counter, and in this new books are displayed with their titles towards the public. It seems to work very well, and has been used with success at Birmingham, Lambeth, and elsewhere, to make known different classes of literature which are not so popular as they should be. Liverpool has, or had, a series of frames in which were movable blocks carrying the titles of additions, and at Rotherham a somewhat similar plan has been adopted. Cardiff shows additions in a frame holding title cards which can be removed by readers and handed over the counter as demand notes. Guard-books like those in use at the British Museum are common, both for additions and general catalogues ; while cards or leaves in volumes laced on cords or rods have been used at Manchester, in Italy, and generally in Europe and America. A neat box with falling sides for holding catalogue cards is used in the University Library of Giessen in Germany, and seems well adapted for staff use, or for private and proprietary libraries. Latest of all is the ingenious cylindrical catalogue-holder or stand invented by Mr. Mason, of St. Martin-in-the-Fields, London. It consists of a broad revolving cylinder, upon the outer rim of which are placed a number of wooden bars, each wide enough to take a written or printed author and title entry. These bars are movable, being designed to slide round the whole circumference of the cylinder, so that additions can be inserted at any part of the alphabet. Each bar represents a book-title, and the plan of using is that the titles of additions should be mounted on the bars, leaving spaces for additions, and so afford a convenient and easily worked accession list in strict alphabetical order. The cylinder is intended to be fixed in a counter front or special stand, and to be all covered in with the exception of a portion about equal to the size of a demy octavo page, which will show under glass. The reader turns the cylinder round to the part of the alphabet he wants by simply turning a handle, and so the whole is shown to him without any waste of public space.

COPYING MACHINES.

Typewriters for cataloguing or listing purposes are making slow progress in public libraries ; but it is unquestionable that before long they will be introduced into every large library. Their advantages are many, among them being greater speed, neatness, and clearness ; not to speak of the attention always bestowed by the public on printed titles or notices as compared with written ones. If many copies of a list of " books wanted " should be required, the typewriter will make a stencil on waxed paper from which can be printed hundreds of copies. If three or six copies of any title or document are required the typewriter will print them all at once. For card-catalogues it is better to print two or three copies of a title at once, and mount them on cards afterwards, making one the author and another the subject entry. The best machines are those called "type-bar" writers, the principle of which is that a circle or row of rods carrying types at the ends, operated by a key like a pianoforte, is made to strike on a common centre, so that a piece of paper fastened at the point of contact is printed by being simply jerked along. The various mechanical devices employed to achieve the different requirements of printing are ingenious, but vary more or less in every machine. The following machines are recommended for trial before a choice is made: the Bar-lock, the Caligraph, the Hammond, the Remington, and the Yost. Any of the manufacturers or agents will allow a week or fortnight's free trial of the machines, and this is the most satisfactory way of deciding. Recommendations of friends and agents alike should be ignored, and the librarian should trust to his own liking in the matter. After all is said, there is really very little difference, as regards cost and manipulation, in the best machines, and the matter resolves itself into a question of meeting the requirements of a particular operator or purpose. In the Bar-lock the type-bars strike downwards through a narrow inked ribbon. There is a separate key for each type. In the Caligraph the bars strike upwards through a broad ink ribbon, and the key-board is arranged with capitals down each side and the lower case letters in the middle. The Hammond is not a type-bar machine, but has two sizes of type on different holders which are exchangeable and is operated by keys carrying the names of two or three letters. The type-holder is struck by a striker working from behind, and the letter is impressed on the paper through an inked ribbon. The keys alter the position of the holder to bring the proper letter or figure against the striker. Cards can be printed more easily by the Hammond than by the other machines. The Remington, which has had the longest career, has a single key-board, each key representing two letters or figures. The bars strike upwards, and the construction of the instrument is excellent. The Yost is a light and compact machine, which prints direct from an ink pad on to the paper. It has a separate key for each type, and a very good arrangement for spacing or inserting missed letters.

Other copying or manifolding machines for manuscript are the Cyclostyle, Mimeograph, and Trypograph. The two former are perhaps most useful in libraries; the Mimeograph being best for manifolding along with the typewriter. The ordinary screw letter copying press is a necessary adjunct of every librarian's office, but in libraries with small incomes an "Anchor" copying press, costing about 12s. 6d., will be found to serve all ordinary purposes.

FILES, BOXES, BOOK-HOLDERS, STAMPS, &c.

Letter files are made in a great variety of styles, from the spiked wire to the elaborate and systematic index of the Amberg and Shannon Companies. A useful series of cheap document files are made by Messrs. John Walker & Co. of London, and comprise manilla paper and cloth envelope, and box files for alphabetical arrangement, to hold papers about 11 × 9 inches, &c. The collapsing accordion files are also made by this firm. Single alphabetical files to hold some hundreds of documents are supplied by the Amberg and Shannon File Companies in neat box form at a small cost; and both these makers can supply file-cabinets of any size or for any purpose, so far as the preservation of documents is concerned. Any of the above-named are preferable to the ordinary wire and binder files which pierce and tear documents without keeping them in get-at-able order. Sheet-music and prints are best preserved in flat boxes with lids and falling fronts, though the former, if kept at all, is best bound in volumes. Print boxes are preferable to portfolios because they are not so apt to crush their contents, and certainly afford a better protection from dust. Pamphlet boxes are made in many styles: some with hinged lids and falling fronts as in the illustration, Fig. 11 ; some with book-shaped backs and hinged ends, and others in two parts.

Most librarians prefer the cloth-covered box with hinged lid and falling front, which can be made in any form by all box-makers. The kind shown in the illustration above are manu-factured by Messrs. Fincham & Co. of London; but others with a uniformly-sized rim are made in Glasgow, Bradford, and Man-chester. Messrs. Marlborough & Co. of London supply boxes made in two parts. For filing unbound magazines and serials the cloth-covered boxes with lids and flaps are most convenient. They should be made of wood when intended for large periodicals like the *Graphic* or *Era*. American cloth or canvas wrappers are sometimes used for preserving periodicals previous to binding, but boxes will, in the long run, be found most economical, cleanly and easily used. There are various kinds of binders made for holding a year's numbers of certain periodicals, in which the

FIG. 11.

parts are either laced with cords or secured by wires to the back. The difficulty with these seems to be that necessary expansion is not always provided against by the appliances supplied. Newspapers intended for binding are usually kept on racks and pro-tected from dust by American cloth or pasteboard wrappers. In

FIG. 12.

other cases a month's papers are laced on perforated wooden bars and kept in rolls.

Stitching machines are sometimes used for periodicals, and though probably quicker than ordinary needle and thread sewing, have certain drawbacks which make their use worthy of some deliberation. In the first place a good machine is expensive, and somewhat liable to get out of order, and in the second place the wires used for the stitching very often rust, and cause much trouble to the binder both because of the tearing of the periodicals and the difficulty of their removal.

Reference might be made here to the "Fauntleroy" magazine case designed by Mr. Chivers of Bath, in which an ingenious and

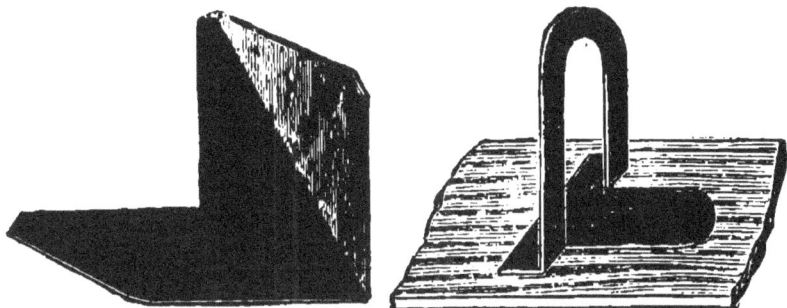

FIGS. 13-14.

neat brass fastener is substituted for elastic or leather thongs.

Application forms are sometimes strung in bundles and left hanging or lying about, but boxes made to their size and provided with thumb-holes in the sides will be found more convenient

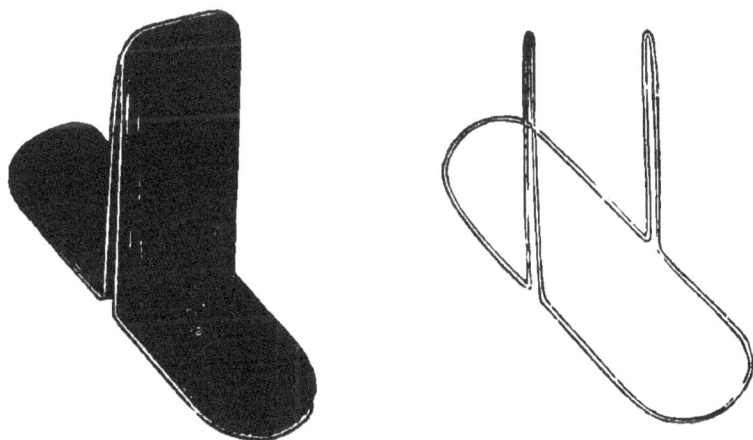

FIGS. 15-16.

and tidy. Various sorts of holders are made for keeping books erect on the shelves or on tables, among which the kinds illustrated above are probably best known. The one shown in Fig. 12, manufactured by Walker & Co. of London, makes an extremely useful device for arranging cards or slips, as it can be adjusted to any space from $\frac{1}{4}$ of an inch. The others are best

adapted for ordinary shelf use.   Figs. 13-14 are made by Messrs.
Braby & Co. of Deptford, London, and Messrs. Lewis & Grundy
of Nottingham.   Figs. 15-16 were designed by Mr. Mason, one
of the secretaries of the Library Association, and are supplied by
Messrs. Wake & Dean of London.

STAMPS, SEALS, &c.

In addition to labels on the boards, it is usual in public libraries
to stamp the name of the institution on certain fixed places
throughout books, in order to simplify identification in cases of
loss, and to deter intending pilferers from stealing.   Metal and
rubber ink stamps have been in use for a long time, and are
doubtless the simplest to apply and cheapest to procure.   The
ordinary aniline inks supplied with these stamps are not reliable,
as they can be quite easily removed by the aid of various
chemicals.   The best ink for the purpose which can be used is
printing ink, but unfortunately it is difficult to apply and takes a
very long time to dry thoroughly.   The best substitute appears to
be the ink for rubber stamps manufactured by Messrs. Stephens
of London, which is not by any means so easily removed as
the purely aniline kinds.   Embossing stamps are perhaps
more satisfactory as regards indelibility than any of those just
mentioned, but they are generally somewhat clumsy in make and
slow in application.   The best method of marking books to
indicate proprietorship and to insure impossibility of removal is
by the use of a perforating stamp, which will bite several pages
at once without disfiguring the book.   Most of the kinds at
present made are rather awkward, but there seems no reason
why a handy perforator in the shape of a pair of pincers should not
be well within the mechanical abilities of the average embossing
stamp maker.   The difficulty with perforating stamps will always
be that of having sufficient points to make the letters clear
without being too large.   Dating stamps for lending library
labels can be had in revolving form for continuous use, or in
small galleys which can be altered from day to day.   The latter
are cheaper and more easily applied.   Seals for public library
Boards which are incorporated can be procured of any engraver
at prices ranging from £5 to £50 according to design and
elaboration.   Those in lever presses are just as effective as those
in screw presses.

LADDERS, &c.

Ladders should always be shod with rubber or leather at the foot to prevent slipping, and an arrangement like that shown in the illustration will be found of service in preventing books from being pushed back in the shelves. The hinged top and top shelf are the invention of Mr. MacAlister, one of the secretaries of the Library Association, and the shelf for the books being replaced or taken down was first used at the Kensington

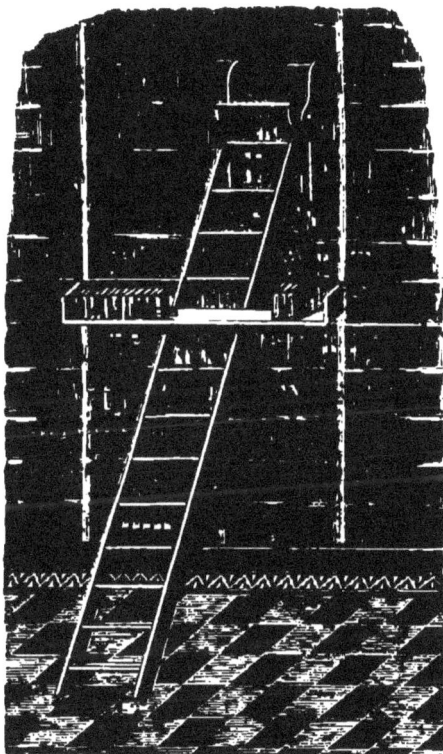

FIG. 17.

Public Library, London. If steps are used instead of ladders they should be made with treads on both sides so that assistants need not turn them about before using. Lightness is a very desirable quality both in steps and ladders, and should be aimed at before durability. There is nothing more tiresome than having to drag about a heavy pair of steps, and the assistants who are entirely free from them have to be congratulated.

In some large libraries trucks are used for the conveyance of heavy volumes. The light truck, covered with leather on the surfaces where books rest, such as is used in the British Museum, will be found very useful. Reference might be made here to the ingenious carrier invented by Miss James of the People's Palace Library, London, for the purpose of conveying books from the galleries to the service counter in the middle of the floor. This consists of a box running on a wire cable, and worked by means of an endless cord and a wheel. For the peculiar purpose for which it was designed it seems to be very satisfactory. There are many other forms of lifts in use for lowering books from galleries, but very few of them are of general application. In certain parishes in London enamelled iron tablets directing to the library have been suspended from the ladder-bars of the street lamps, to show strangers the whereabouts of the institution. These are effective as a means of advertising the library, and might be used for a similar purpose in all large towns.

BOOKS OF RECORD.

For maintaining a permanent register of the different kinds of work accomplished in libraries a great number of books are used, the varieties of which are as numerous as charging systems. It would serve no useful purpose to describe all of these books, much less their variations, and so we shall content ourselves by taking a few typical specimens as representative of all the rest. As the names of these various books sufficiently describe their purpose, it will only be necessary to briefly indicate the uses of the more obscure kinds and give occasional rulings in explanation of the others.

The **minute book** contains a complete history of the work of the library as far as the proceedings of the Library Board is concerned, and in many cases it is really a succinct record of all the most important operations of the institution. It should be well bound in morocco or other strong leather, and should consist of good quality paper ruled faint and margin, and paged. The **agenda book** forms the necessary accompaniment of the minutes, and is a sort of draft minute book in which all the business to come before the meeting is entered. A plain foolscap folio book, ruled faint only, will serve for this purpose. The business is generally entered on one side of the folio and the resolutions of the meeting on the other. To save possible misunderstandings the chairman ought to enter the decisions of the Board himself, after reading them over, and the minutes should be compiled from this record rather than from separate notes made by the clerk. The business books of public libraries are not often kept by the librarian, except in London where the duties of clerk are usually conjoined. For that reason it is perhaps needless to do more than name the cash book, ledger, petty cash book, cash receipt book, and postage book as the principal records maintained for financial purposes. Many librarians unite their issue and receipts from fines books, while others keep separate records; but it is best for beginners to keep their cash affairs strictly apart, and in the ordinary fashion of good business houses. The **donation book** is the record of all books, prints, maps, or other gifts to the library, ruled to show the following particulars : Author and Title | Vols. and Date | Name and Address of Donor | Date of Receipt | Date of Acknowledgment | and, sometimes, the library number. Some libraries have this book with a counterfoil, in which a double entry is made, and the detachable portion is torn off to form a thanks circular. This is a very convenient style of register.

Proposition book and **suggestion book.** In many cases these are nothing more than plain faint ruled folio volumes, in which readers are allowed to enter suggestions of new books or on the management of the library. Often, however, the proposition book is ruled to carry the following particulars : Book proposed | Publisher and Price | Date of Publication | Name and Address of Proposer | Decision of Committee | Date or Number of Order | . In other cases a form is supplied to readers desirous of making suggestions of any sort. **Contract** or **estimate books** are not always used, but the young librarian will find it of the greatest convenience to keep a chronological record of every estimate received for work to be done in the library. A guard book in which can be pasted the various tenders received, or an ordinary plain ruled one in which they can be entered, will be found a perfect treasury of assistance in many cases. An index at the beginning or end can easily be made. **Inventory books** are intended to furnish a complete record of all the library property, showing when, from whom, and at what cost every item of

furniture, fitting, stationery, &c., was procured. It can be kept in
a specially ruled book, or in a faint ruled folio, classified to show
the different kinds of supplies. When re-ordering or reckoning
up the duration of supplies, this book will be found of the greatest
use. As a record of prices it is also valuable. **Invoice books**
are sometimes kept in two forms : first, as mere guard books in
which paid invoices are pasted; and second, as chronological
records of every lot of books received by purchase or donation.
This very often saves much trouble in fixing the routine in which
books should be dealt with when being prepared for public use.
The ordinary ruling is as follows : Date of Receipt | Name of
Donor or Vendor | First Word of Invoice | No. of Vols. | Total Cost
| Remarks | . In addition to these columns some librarians add
spaces for marking with initials when every process connected
with the preparation of the books has been finished. **Location
books** are used only with the movable system of shelving books
and are long narrow volumes ruled to hold 50 lines on a folio,
with the numbers written or printed down one side, generally
running from 1 to 10,000. The specimen ruling will show this
plainly.

501-550

No.	Location.	Author and Title.
501		
02		
03		

The first new book awaiting treatment of course receives the first
unappropriated number. Some location books give additional
particulars, such as a column for the date of accession of books,
which is often required when spaces are left for continued sets of
a series. The **stock book** in most libraries forms a numerical
catalogue of accessions in the order of their receipt ; giving
particulars of edition, binding, vendor or donor, price, and other
information. It is, therefore, the most valuable record kept
by the library, if the minute book is excepted. Some are
classified, others classify the books in separate columns, while
a few keep the classification in a different book. The following selection of headings will show the variety of rulings

in use. At Bradford a classified stock book is used, and it
is ruled thus :—

(PRESS) 850-899.			CLASS.		
DATE.	BOOK No.	TITLE.	AUTHOR.		STOCK BOOK No.
	850 851 852				

The last column refers to a book in which purchases are entered
with a consecutive numbering, and is an index to the accession of
the volumes, while the stock book shown above is primarily a
place book. It is thus rather a shelf register than a record of
accession of stock. The Mitchell Library, Glasgow, uses the
following headings : Date of Receipt | Author and Title | Lan-
guage | Number | Class Letter | Number of Vols. | New Work or
Continuation | Book or Pamphlet | Size | Place of Publication |
Date of Publication | Condition when Received | Donor, if Pre-
sented | Price, if Purchased | Discount | Vendor | Collation |
Special Collections | Remarks | . Various Modifications of this
stock book are used in different libraries. At Manchester a
much briefer description is given, namely : Date when Received |
Author | Title | No. of Vols. | No. of Pamphlets | Class | Size |
Place of Publication | Date when Published | Condition when
Received | Donor, if Presented | Price, if Purchased | Vendor, if
Purchased | Remarks | . In this book no provision seems to be
made for the number which directs to the place of books or their
order of accession. The stock book used at Lambeth classifies as
it goes along, and has headings as follows : | Stock Number |
                                              | 7501 |
Shelf Number | Author and Title | Volumes | Condition |
   B 1874 | | | |
                                  | How Acquired |
Vendor or Donor | Price | Bought | Given | News Room |
   Classification. | | |
A. B. C. D. E. F. G. H. I. | Remarks | . This is intended for

lending library books. For reference libraries the dates of publication and other particulars of edition would be given. At Liverpool and Chelsea a cumulative system of classifying is used, which is shown in the following sample : | Date Received | Author | Title | No. of Vols. | Size | Place of Publication | Date of Publication | Bound in | Class | Number | Donor or Vendor | Price | Net Total | Class Accession Number | Accession Number | Remarks | .

With stock books of the Glasgow pattern a classification book is commonly used, in which are entered abstracts of classes, books, pamphlets, purchases, gifts, works as distinguished from volumes, special collections, totals, &c., page by page. Accuracy is almost inevitable by this method, owing to the numerous cross checks provided. In some libraries separate stock books are kept for periodicals and annual publications, but the principle in all is similar to the ordinary stock book. It only remains to add that, as stock books are records of some importance and permanency, they ought to be made of the very best materials. The **shelf register**, as the name indicates, is the volume in which a list of the books is kept, in the order of their arrangement on the shelves. Such registers are only required for the fixed plan of location. The most elementary form simply gives the | Press Mark | Author and Title | No. of Vols. | Stock, Progressive, or Consecutive Number | ; the last referring to the entry in the accessions or stock book. Others are much more elaborate, being really varieties of classified stock books, and giving particulars of edition, price, &c. The main uses of the shelf catalogue or register are to fix the numbers of new books, and to afford a ready means of taking stock. The varieties of this book are practically endless, and we shall only give two other specimens :—

Press No....................
Shelf Letter..............

Date of Accession.	Shelf Order.	Progressive Number.	Author.	Short Title	Place.	Date.

and

Remarks.	Number.	Author.	Title of Book.	Admitted.

Duplicate registers give particulars of the accession of duplicate books, and their destination if sold or exchanged. **Order
and letter books** are usually just separate copying books, but
frequently the former are kept with counterfoils, and sometimes
separate ruled forms are used, and simply copied into an ordinary
tissue letter book. **Binding books** or sheets record the volumes
sent out for binding or repair, and usually note the following
particulars :—

Manchester.   Date of Sending.
| Press Mark | Title of Book for Lettering | Date of Return |
Binder's Charge | .

Bradford.   Date of Sending.
| Style | Book Number | Title | Price | .

Mitchell Library, Glasgow.   Date of Sending.
| Instruction | Lettering | Date of Return | .

Borrowers' and **guarantors' registers** are sometimes kept in
books, but often on cards, which are the most convenient. They
register names, addresses, period of borrowing right, and guarantors
in one case, and names, addresses, and persons guaranteed in the
other. In some libraries a record of each borrower's reading is
posted on to his card from the book application forms.

Periodical receipt and check books are for marking off the
current numbers of newspapers and magazines as received from
the newsagent, and for checking them each morning as they lie
on the tables or racks. Ruled sheets and cards are also used for
the same purpose. They usually consist of lists of monthly,
weekly, daily, and other periodicals, with rulings to show dates
of receipt or finding covering a period of one to six months.
Issue books, for recording the issues of books in libraries, are
designed in many styles, each having reference to the particular
requirements of a certain institution. Generally, however, the
particulars preserved include : | Date | No. of Vols. Issued by
Classes | Totals | Weekly or Monthly Average | . Many give
the number of visits to newsrooms and reading-rooms, while others
include the amounts received from fines, sale of catalogues, &c.
One issue book is usually ruled to show the work accomplished
in every department, but many libraries keep separate registers
for lending and reference departments. In towns where there are

a number of branch libraries the returns of issues, &c., are often recorded in a very elaborate and complete fashion. The day book or issue ledger has already been referred to under ledger charging systems, but in addition to these there is an endless variety of daily issue sheets, some simple and some very complex. It would be useless to give patterns of these, as the whole question of their adoption hinges on the main system by which each library is managed. **Work books, time book** and **sheets, scrap books,** and **lost and found registers** are sufficiently described by their names. The two first are for staff management, and in large libraries are absolutely necessary ; the work book for noting the duties of each assistant, and the time book or sheet for recording times of arrival and departure from duty. Lost and found registers record thefts, mutilations, or other abstractions of library property, and dates and descriptions of articles found on the premises. These are, roughly speaking, the most necessary books of record required in the administration of a public library, but many others exist which have been designed for special purposes. The Museum of the Association contains specimens of many of the books above named, and librarians are, as a rule, glad to show what they have in the way of novelties or variations from standard patterns.

FORMS AND STATIONERY.

Here again selection is difficult, owing to the perplexing quantity and variety of forms, and we shall, with as little comment as possible, merely give specimens or indicate uses.

Precept forms are the requisitions for the library rate presented by London Commissioners to the Local Boards or Vestries.

Public notices, rules, &c., should be boldly printed and displayed in glazed frames.

Requisition forms are in use in a few of the larger libraries. They are filled up and submitted to the Library Committee when supplies are wanted. They seem rather a useless formality where an agenda book is kept.

Thanks circulars or *acknowledgment forms* usually bear the arms of the library, and are engraved on quarto sheets of good paper. Many libraries use a simple post-card with a very curt acknowledgment. Others use perforated receipt books or donation books with counterfoils, like those previously described.

Labels and *book-plates* for the inside of the boards of books in addition to the name and arms of the library often bear location marks and book numbers, or the names of donors. Paste holds them better than gum, and is much cleaner. An engraved book-plate of any artistic pretension should be dated and signed by designer and engraver. It is to be regretted that more of our large reference libraries do not use photographic or other reproductions of views of their best rooms for this purpose. The town's arms are inappropriate and meaningless, while the library interior is of historical interest and germane to the object held in view, namely, marking suitably to indicate ownership.

Issues and *rule-labels* are chiefly used in lending libraries, though some reference libraries have labels on which the dates of issues are noted. The issue-labels must be ruled to suit the system of charging adopted, the ledger systems as a rule requiring something more than mere date slips. The rule-labels usually bear an abstract of the library rules applicable to the borrowing of books.

Vouchers for lending library borrowers must, of course, be arranged according to the general rules of the library; but in every case the agreement should take the form of a declaration : " I, the undersigned," or " I,   , do hereby," or " I, of   , ratepayer in the   , do hereby". A large selection of all kinds of these vouchers and applications for the right of borrowing are preserved in the Museum of the Library Association. Most librarians bind the vouchers when filled up and numbered in convenient volumes, or mount them in blank books.

Borrowers' tickets or *cards* also are entirely governed by the system of charging as regards shape, size, and material. Mill-board, pasteboard, leather, wood, and cloth are all used. In cases where borrowers are allowed to retain their cards when they have books out it is advisable to have them rather strongly made, or else provide cases, especially when the right of borrowing extends over two years.

Receipts for fines, &c., may either be in books of numbered and priced tickets—1d., 2d., 3d., 6d., &c.—or in perforated counterfoil books with running numbers. Both kinds are extensively used, as well as tissue books with carbonised paper, similar to those seen in drapers' shops.

Application forms for books exist in many varieties, but chiefly in connection with reference libraries. The number of lending libraries which use the application slips is as yet comparatively small, but there are indications pointing to a more general adoption of this appliance, especially where indicators are used. Some reference libraries have an elaborate application in duplicate, one part being retained when the transaction is complete, and the other returned to the borrower. The plan adopted in the British Museum of charging assistants with issues, and returning the readers' applications, is not recommended for imitation. The very special arrangements of the Museum require special means of working, which are not suitable for general adoption. On reference library applications, in addition to the usual admonitory sentences as to books being only for use on the premises, &c., it is customary to ask for the book number or its press mark, author and title, volumes wanted, reader's name and address, and date. In addition most libraries include a space for the initials of the assistant who issues and replaces the book, while some ask for the ages and professions of readers. Lending library applications need be no more elaborate than this:—

—————— PUBLIC LIBRARY.	
No. OF BOOK WANTED.	No. OF BORROWER'S TICKET.
	DATE.

Or this:—

—————— PUBLIC LIBRARY.
LENDING DEPARTMENT.

BOOK NUMBER.	AUTHOR AND TITLE OF BOOK WANTED.	TICKET NUMBER.
	DATE.	VOLS. ISSUED,

Renewal slips and post-cards, and bespoke cards or forms require no description.

Information circulars and *readers' handbooks* are becoming more and more general, and many useful documents of the kind have been issued. The object of all is to direct attention to the library, its uses, and contents, while making more public the rules, newspapers taken, hours of opening, &c. The little handbooks issued from Manchester, Boston (U.S.), Glasgow, and elsewhere, are models.

The barest reference will suffice for such articles as bookmarks, cloth or paper, overdue notices and post-cards, issue returns, branch library returns, infectious diseases notification forms, and stock-taking returns, all of which are almost explained by their names. It should be stated as a curious fact that very many persons object to having notices of overdue books or defaulting borrowers sent on post-cards, while others think a charge for the postage of such notices an imposition. Any young librarian desirous of obtaining specimens of these or any other forms will always be sure to get them on application at the various libraries. The Museum, as before stated, contains a number of all kinds of forms.

As regards ordinary STATIONERY it is hardly necessary to say much. Note-paper is usually stamped with the library arms, and envelopes with the name on the flap. Pens, ink, pencils, rulers, date-cases, paper-knives, &c., are all so familiar that it would be waste of time to consider them separately. Any intelligent librarian will find endless suggestion and profit from a visit to a large stationer's warehouse, and may even pick up wrinkles of some value by keeping his eyes open to the adaptability of many articles of manufactured stationery.

RECIPES.

Pastes. Ordinary flour paste is made by mixing flour and water to the consistency of a thin cream, taking care that all knots are rubbed out, and boiling over a slow fire with constant stirring until it becomes translucent. It can be made of almost any thickness and toughness, and by the admixture of a little glue very strong paste is obtained. A few drops of oil of cloves, creasote, or corrosive sublimate, or a few grains of salicylic acid

INDEX.

ABERDEEN UNIVERSITY PRESS.